DARNELL P. SMITH

AWAKENING THE NIGHT

Copyright © 2024 Darnell P. Smith

All rights reserved.

ISBN: 979-8-9906786-2-0

This book is dedicated to our Earth mother, who gave us life and the opportunity to be. May we strive to honor her as devoted children should, working to restore balance and peace. As we heal ourselves, we lighten her load. No longer must she carry the weight of it all. Let us help heal her, ensuring she feels safe and cared for, as every blessed child is called to do. May we aid in lifting her burdens, allowing her to release and let go of all of her woes.

A special thanks to my wife Sherniece Johnson Smith for the artwork she created and bringing my cover photo's vision to life. And to my dear friend Chelsey J. Macklin for assembling these pages, helping them to effortlessly flow.

ACKNOWLEDGMENTS

On this journey of becoming, as I ventured into adolescence, the first real teacher to awaken something within me was Abiodun Oyewole. Our engagement did not occur in a traditional classroom but during my first summer youth employment, where Brother Abiodun was one of the instructors teaching Creative Writing. At the time, I had no idea who he was or the influence he had on Hip Hop culture. To me, he was simply a man with a commanding presence, skillfully playing with words in a deeply cultural context. His poetry ignited a spark within me, creating the impetus for me to push past my fears. In the dark nights of self-doubt, he was one of the first lights I encountered, leaving a profound impact on my life. Another pivotal figure in my journey was Louis Watkins, the Youth Service Coordinator, who invited me to serve as a youth representative on our local community board. He did not see me as invisible. Instead, he recognized something valuable within me and created opportunities for me to grow. Through this process, I learned about the frailties of politics, how to engage with adults and the media, and even experienced travel abroad. Had he not taken a chance on me, my path might have been very different. From my involvement in youth services, I was later influenced by a man I greatly admired, who embodied care, concern, and upliftment. He showed me what it meant to be part of government in a way I had never seen before or since. He was the first person I ever heard use the term African American. Leonard Dunston was more than just a former

Commissioner of the NYS Division for Youth. He was a model of manhood. His presence left an indelible mark on my heart. Choosing to attend college was a step in a new direction. I sought to go to a Black institution and my experience there assessed my resilience. Coming from New York to what was considered one of the best HBCU's in the country, I quickly realized there were no singular "Black institutions." If one truly existed, it could have altered our condition. The only faculty member to ever offer me encouragement in a meaningful way was Dr. Alan Colon. He challenged us to embrace our culture in ways that the institution itself never did. Lastly, I must acknowledge William Griggs, author of *The Megalight Connection*, which is one of my all-time favorite books. Bill inspired me to think outside of the box, to dig deeper, and to reexamine the condition of people of African descent from new perspectives. After reading his book, I sought him out, before the convenience of cell phones existed, to connect with someone whose ideas had profoundly shaped my thinking. I am fortunate to have had the guidance of my father, grandfathers, uncles, and the distinguished men I have mentioned above. What makes these men truly remarkable is that they had no obligation to invest in me, yet they did. It was out of the pure spirit of leadership and mentorship.

    I wish to express my heartfelt gratitude to Ms. Joan Ann Bostic as well, whose unwavering support has been instrumental in my journey. Her encouragement and belief in my work have been a source of strength. I am deeply thankful for her presence through this process.

AWAKENINING THE NIGHT: DARNELL P. SMITH

FOREWORD

BISMILLAH. I've been blessed to know Darnell Smith since 1971 in a sibling-like relationship. I have watched him develop into a true humanitarian that authentically champions the rights of the fallen. He has always had a sincere admiration for humanity, and I've been very blessed/fortunate to personally benefit from his mentorship during my lengthy period of incarceration and beyond. When I was informed that he'd be writing another book, I was very elated! Darnell has definitely done many great things in the world, and I wholeheartedly believe that this particular book will inspire readers to develop the courage to go after their dreams and assiduously strive towards making a positive impact in society. Darnell's book shows how readers can recognize their struggles, validate their feelings, while offering support and reminding them of their strengths and the power of resilience.

Jamaal Umar Abdur-Rahman
(*formerly known as Roger V. Smith, II*)

"Throughout life, I've experienced the ebb and flow of financial loss, as if it arrived in seasons, each episode more challenging than the last. Almost like an illness that can consume, pushing you to make impulsive decisions rather than those that are well-informed. Once that mindset takes hold, patience vanishes, and the fear of hitting rock bottom keeps you from making rational choices. However, if we find the strength to pause for a moment and accept our setbacks, we might realize that loss is entwined with a peculiar sensation. A sensation we unwittingly start to crave."

— . . o) .☉. ☾ o . . —

"The sensation of loss is a spirit we often embrace, inviting it to reside within us. To experience the exhilaration of victory, we must venture beyond our existing knowledge, traumas, and fears, all of which we have become intimately familiar with. The sea of success lies tantalizingly within reach, awaiting our grasp. All it takes is the exercise of our keen sense of awareness and the courage to move beyond our fears, where the spirit of true victory thrives."

─── . . o ☽ ⚬ ☾ o . . ───

"In this realm, abundance and wealth abound, but it is not an uncharted territory. There are rules to financial success by which we must diligently abide. These rules are the guiding principles that steer us toward prosperity. They include financial discipline, smart investments, and a commitment to continuous learning."

─── . . o ☽ ⚬ ☾ o . . ───

"To discover this guiding beacon of hope, we must follow an inner light, which is our intuition and passion for what we do. It is this internal compass that helps us navigate the complex waters of success, even when faced with storms of doubt and adversity. We must remain unwavering in our determination and never lose sight of our goals."

——— · · o ☽ ·☼· ☾ o · · ———

"Success is not a destination but a journey, filled with difficulties. It requires resilience, adaptability, and a mindset that embraces failure as a stepping stone to growth. By persistently pushing past our comfort zones and embracing change, we unlock the doors to where our dreams and aspirations become reality."

─── · · o) ·ọ· ☾ o · · ───

"In the end, the path to success is not always smooth, but it is in the face of challenges that we truly discover our potential. Let us not only invite the spirit of victory but also nurture it, for within it lies the abundant rewards we seek."

─── · · o) ·ọ· ☾ o · · ───

"How are you riding the rails of your life? I find solace in prayer, embodying presence, resilience, confidence, and balance. Prayer connects me to a higher power, providing guidance and support along my journey. Being present allows me to fully engage each moment, savoring its beauty and learning from its lessons. With resilience, I bounce back from challenges, using setbacks as opportunities for growth. Confidence fuels my belief in myself and my abilities, empowering me to pursue my dreams fearlessly. Through balance, I harmonize the various aspects of life, ensuring that no area is neglected. As I ride the rails of life, I embrace these qualities, trusting in their transformative power to guide me towards a fulfilling, purposeful existence."

"Failure and defeat may bring bitterness, but it is the sting of betrayal that inflicts a deeper wound. Like a broken blade thrust into the back, its point pierces the heart and sows the seed of hatred. From this barren desert of despair, this seed germinates, taking the shape of a resilient cactus, reminding us of the pain endured. Let us strive for loyalty and trust, nurturing an oasis of compassion where swords remain sheathed and hearts remain untainted."

---   · · ○ ☽ ☉ ☾ ○ · ·   ---

"What manner of man are we if we are bestowed with the gift of sight, yet remain blind to the truths that surround us? Let us open our eyes to the world's beauty, its sorrows, and its mysteries. Only then can we truly understand our purpose and embrace the wonders that await us."

---   · · ○ ☽ ☉ ☾ ○ · ·   ---

"The greatest victory of your life has already been achieved, and you hold the crown of triumph upon your very existence. Each and every one of you can

proudly bestow upon
yourselves a medal of
honor. Look around you, for
you are surrounded by
fellow champions. Now, you
may wonder, what grand
competition did I conquer
to earn such accolades? The
answer lies in the very
essence of your being. It
is your birth!

You emerged triumphant in a
fierce race against 250
million other sperm cells,
all vying to fertilize the
egg within your mother.
This competition, the
journey to conception, is
the most extraordinary and
significant battle any of
us will ever face. In that
moment, you emerged as the

ultimate victor, destined to embark upon a unique path of life."

―― · · o ☽ ·○· ☾ o · · ――

"Embrace the magnitude of your victory, for it is a testament to your strength, resilience, and the infinite possibilities that reside within you. Wear your crown with pride, for you are a living testament to the remarkable power of life itself. Let this realization ignite a fire within you, fueling your determination to make the most of the precious gift you have been given. Remember, you are a champion from the very beginning, and your life is a testament to your extraordinary triumph."

——— · · o ☽ ⋄ ☾ o · · ———

"Love is luminescence, illuminating our paths with its radiant glow. It is weightless, liberating us from the shackles of fear and judgment. Love is the ultimate binding force, uniting souls in a cosmic dance of connection, yet it never seeks to confine or imprison. It is an energy that knows no bounds, flowing freely between hearts and souls."

——— · · o ☽ ⋄ ☾ o · · ———

"Letting go is not an act

of forgetting, but a powerful act of liberation. It is the act of transcending the clutches of those who have intentionally sought to diminish your worth and keep you confined to their level. It is a courageous choice to rise above their influence and reclaim your own power and self-worth.

When you let go, you release the chains that have bound you to their limited perceptions and judgments. You break free from the weight of their expectations and manipulations. It is an act of reclaiming your authenticity and embracing your own path.

Letting go empowers you to soar higher, beyond the limitations that others have imposed upon you. It allows you to redefine your own narrative, to forge your own destiny, and to discover the limitless possibilities that await you.

Let go with grace and strength. Rise above the grasp of those who seek to diminish your light. Embrace your own worth and step into a realm of freedom and self-discovery. Remember, letting go is not a sign of weakness, but a testament to your resilience and ability to transcend the negativity that others may try to impose upon you."

——— . . o) ·☉· (o . . ———

"Being an accountant is akin to mastering the art of navigating the intricate balance between the positives and negatives that life presents. It is understood that experiencing deficits does not equate to true loss, but rather an opportunity for growth and learning. Sometimes, the greatest lessons are forged through the fires of hardship, forging us into stronger and wiser individuals.

In those areas where

deficits have crossed your path, lies the potential for you to uncover your greatest strengths. Embrace the challenges, for they hold the keys to unlocking your hidden potential. Push forward with determination, keeping a watchful eye on the lessons that unfold before you.

Just like a skilled accountant, seize the chance to profit from both your mistakes and accomplishments. Embrace the wisdom gained from your missteps and celebrate the victories that come your way. Remember, it is through the harmonious integration of gains and losses that we find balance and move closer to our fullest potential.

Be an exceptional accountant in your own life. Embrace the journey, both the triumphs and setbacks, for they shape you into the resilient, capable individual you are meant to become. May you thrive and flourish in all that you pursue. Be well!"

―― · · ○ ☽ ·☉· ☾ ○ · · ――

"These profound questions we conjure speak to the longing for personal and collective redemption, a yearning to transcend our flaws and find a path towards healing and liberation."

─ · · o ☽ ⚬̇ ☾ o · · ─

"To get right, we must first acknowledge and confront the stains on our hands: the wrongs we have committed, the harm we may have caused. It requires a deep examination of our actions, motives, and values, and a willingness to take responsibility for our shortcomings. Through self-reflection, we can begin the process of self-improvement and growth."

─ · · o ☽ ⚬̇ ☾ o · · ─

"Cleaning our blood-stained hands is a metaphorical journey of purification. It involves seeking forgiveness, both from others and ourselves, and actively working towards making amends and restitution. It requires sincere efforts to change harmful behaviors and to cultivate empathy, compassion, and understanding."

— · · o ☽ ·☼· ☾ o · · —

"Freeing ourselves entails breaking free from the chains of past mistakes, traumas, and negative patterns. It involves embracing forgiveness, letting go of grudges and resentment, and finding the courage to move forward with renewed purpose and clarity. Inner liberation also involves confronting our fears, insecurities, and limiting beliefs, and finding the strength to overcome them.

Climbing out of the metaphorical hole we have fallen into requires resilience and perseverance. It demands a commitment to personal growth, seeking support and guidance when needed, and finding the determination to rise above our challenges. It may involve seeking help from trusted friends, mentors, or professionals who can provide guidance and support along the way."

― . . o ☽ ·ọ· ☾ o . . ―

"Ultimately, the journey towards getting right, cleaning our hands, freeing ourselves, and climbing out of the hole is a deeply personal and ongoing process. It requires introspection, self-compassion, and a commitment to continuous growth and self-improvement. With dedication and a genuine desire for transformation, we can embark on a path of healing and rise to new heights of self-realization and fulfillment."

"In a society often plagued by self-interest and indifference, acts of kindness stand as beacons of light, illuminating the paths of those in need. They remind us of our shared humanity, restoring faith in the goodness that resides within each of us.

May we never take these acts for granted, but rather, cherish them as the catalysts for positive change that they are. Together, let us cultivate a culture of kindness, where acts of love and compassion become the norm rather than the exception."

"Become a change agent and a catalyst for transformation. Embrace your higher vibration, that elevated state of consciousness, and witness the profound impact it has on the world around you. As you undergo your own personal transition, you become a beacon of light, radiating positivity and inspiration."

"By embodying your authentic self and embracing your true potential, you inspire others to do the same. Your elevated energy and positive mindset create a ripple effect, touching the lives of those around you. Your presence alone becomes a catalyst for change, as people are drawn to the authenticity and vibrancy you exude."

―― · · o ☽ ⚬̇ ☾ o · · ――

"Through your actions, words, and intentions, you have the power to ignite a spark within others. You plant seeds of possibility and empower them to embark on their own transformative journeys. As they awaken to their true selves, the collective energy shifts, and a wave of positive change sweeps through the world."

"Embrace your higher vibration and let it radiate outward. Be a living example of love, compassion, and empowerment. Trust in the transformative power you possess and watch as the world responds to your authentic expression. Together, we can create a ripple of change that transcends boundaries and elevates collective consciousness."

"There is both danger in

knowing and danger in not knowing. It is in raising your vibration, elevating your consciousness, that you gain the ability to navigate through the intricate jungle of life. As you increase your vibrational frequency, you become more attuned to the energies and vibrations that surround you.

In this heightened state of awareness, you develop a discerning eye, capable of distinguishing the healthy fruit from that which has been poisoned. You see beyond the surface, beyond illusions, and tap into a deeper wisdom that guides your choices and actions.

Your intuition becomes sharper, and you align yourself with experiences, people, and situations that are in harmony with your well-being."

―― . . o) .ọ. (o . . ――

"Raise your vibration and venture forth into the jungle of life with an open heart and a discerning mind. Embrace the transformative power that comes with a heightened state of consciousness. By doing so, you navigate through challenges with grace, uncover hidden truths, and forge a path that aligns with your highest self. Trust in your ability to discern and let your elevated vibration guide you towards a life of fulfillment and purpose."

—— . . o ☽ ☉ ☾ o . . ——

"If there is one commitment worth making, let it be the commitment to love yourself more. Embrace the journey of self-love, forgiveness, and acceptance. See your imperfections not as weaknesses, but as unique gifts bestowed upon you by the Creator. These flaws are intended to keep you humble, reminding you of your purpose and mission in life."

—— . . o ☽ ☉ ☾ o . . ——

"Commit to recognizing the profound gift and the healing essence you bring to the world. Understand that the world needs your presence, your authentic self, and the unique medicine you carry within. By committing to yourself, you honor your own worthiness and acknowledge the profound impact you can make. In this commitment, embrace the journey of self-discovery and self-acceptance. Forgive yourself for past mistakes, knowing that they have shaped you and propelled you forward. Embrace your imperfections as opportunities for growth and learning. By loving and accepting yourself, you cultivate a deep sense of inner peace and fulfillment."

——— · · ○ ☽ ·☉· ☾ ○ · · ———

"Remember, committing to yourself is not selfish; it is an act of self-care and empowerment. It is through nurturing your own well-being that you can truly show up for others and make a positive difference in the world. So, commit to yourself, commit to your growth, and commit to honoring the beautiful soul that you are. Embrace the journey of self-love, and watch as your light shines brighter, illuminating the path for yourself and others."

── . . o ☽ ☌ ☾ o . . ──

"Instead of constantly stepping down and resisting change, it is often more empowering and fruitful to step up and embrace it. Change is an inevitable part of life, and by embracing it, we open ourselves to new opportunities, growth, and personal transformation.

When we step up and embrace change, we adopt a proactive mindset. We recognize that change can be a catalyst for positive outcomes and personal development. Instead of fearing the unknown, we approach it with curiosity and a willingness to learn and adapt.

Embracing change requires us to let go of old patterns and beliefs that hold us back. It invites us to challenge ourselves, step out of our comfort zones, and explore new possibilities. By doing so, we expand our horizons and discover untapped potential within ourselves.

Stepping up and embracing change also enables us to become more resilient and adaptable. We learn to navigate through life's uncertainties and challenges with greater ease, recognizing that change often brings valuable lessons and opportunities for growth.

Furthermore, embracing change can lead to personal fulfillment and a deeper sense of purpose. It allows us to align ourselves with our authentic desires and values, enabling us to create a life that truly resonates with who we are.

Instead of always stepping down and resisting change, consider stepping up and embracing it. Embrace the opportunities it presents, the growth it facilitates, and the transformation it can bring. By doing so, you empower yourself to live a more fulfilling and meaningful life."

―― · · o ☽ ⚲ ☾ o · · ――

"When you see beyond the surface, you discover the richness and depth that lies within. It is in this space that understanding, empathy, and genuine connection flourish. By seeing beyond the image and acknowledging the multifaceted nature of an individual, you embark on a journey of truly seeing and knowing."

―― · · o ☽ ⚲ ☾ o · · ――

"When we prioritize work solely for the sake of survival, without pursuing

our passions, we
inadvertently surrender our
freedom. Each day, work
consumes precious time,
stealing moments that could
be devoted to what truly
brings us joy. If we view
this loss as a theft, let
it be something we
collectively yearn to
reclaim: time itself.

―― · · o ☽ ·☼· ☾ o · · ――

"While work is an essential
part of our lives, it
should not overshadow the
importance of quality time
with those who hold
significance in our hearts.
Let us strive to strike a
balance, reclaiming stolen
moments and creating space

for the relationships that bring us joy, love, and a true sense of fulfillment."

—— . . o ☽ ·☼· ☾ o . . ——

"Engaging in conversations that highlight people's knowledge fosters a sense of empowerment and encourages a sharing of ideas. It allows individuals to contribute their expertise and helps to cultivate a culture of mutual learning and growth.

Remember that everyone has something valuable to offer and, by focusing on what they do know, we can foster an environment that nurtures collaboration, understanding, and the expansion of knowledge for all involved."

——— . . o) .ọ. ☾ o . . ———

"Embrace the art of lightening your load and releasing the burdensome rocks that obstruct your path. These challenges were never intended for you to carry indefinitely, but rather as stepping stones on your journey towards growth and resilience. Lift them with determination, extracting the valuable lessons they offer, and then set them aside. For it is in the act of freeing yourself from their weight that you truly gain strength, clearing the way to embrace new opportunities and a lighter, more liberated existence."

── . . o ☽ ⭒ ☾ o . . ──

"What have you attached yourself to? Who or what lifts you up? Who or what brings you down? Why do you so quickly sever the connection to who and what you love? Why do you cement yourself to what weighs you down? Life's tapestry is woven with our choices of attachment, where threads of joy and purpose intertwine. Seek those who lift your spirits, like the air beneath your wings, propelling you to new heights of inspiration and growth. Embrace the love that binds your heart, nurturing its roots with tender care. But beware, for amidst the ebb and flow, there may be anchors that weigh you down.

Reflect upon them, for they may hold valuable lessons or serve as catalysts for change. Let wisdom guide your discernment, allowing you to selectively weave your connections, embracing what fuels your soul and gracefully shedding what hinders your ascent to a life of fulfillment and bliss."

"You are the application being meticulously programmed, shaped by your experiences and choices. Just like any device, your potential output is influenced by the limitations inherent in your design. Consider this: if you continually feed your mind and spirit with negativity and worthless input, what outcome should you truly expect? Unless you embrace the transformative power of alchemy, wherein you transmute the negative into the positive, inputting garbage will invariably yield garbage as output. The key lies in consciously selecting the nourishment you provide to your being, for it is through intentional choices and uplifting input that you unlock the potential for growth, transformation, and the manifestation of your highest self."

─── . . o) .ȯ. (o . . ───

"When life assumes the role of your teacher, embrace the wisdom of being receptive to discovering opportunities within moments of turmoil. Not every upset signifies a definitive defeat, and not every victory guarantees an outright win. Look beyond the surface, for within the difficulties of existence lie valuable lessons waiting to be unraveled. Open your heart and mind to the hidden potentials that can transform setbacks into stepping stones and reveal profound insights that transcend conventional notions of success and failure."

───   · · o ☽ ·☼· ☾ o · ·   ───

"True victory transcends mere triumph; it lies not solely in the act of winning, but in how one navigates the depths of defeat. It is through the crucible of loss that the essence of genuine victory emerges. Only by tasting the bitterness of defeat can one truly savor the sweetness of triumph, discerning the stark contrast between the two. It is in this profound understanding that the essence of true victory takes root and flourishes."

─── . • o ☽ ·☼· ☾ o • . ───

"As you gaze into the mirror, treat the figure before you with tenderness and compassion. Cease the self-abuse, release the doubts that plague your mind. The reflection you see is deserving of your love, kindness, and forgiveness. Remember, you are a Co-Creator of the magnificent vessel that houses your essence. There exists no flaw in your intricate design. Embrace gratitude and grant yourself permission to let your inner light radiate brightly, illuminating the world around you."

──— . . o ☽ .☌. ☾ o . . ───

"Love is inherently meant to be effortless, unburdened by expectations, demands, desires, and wants. Love is a radiant and nourishing force that uplifts you rather than weighs you down. When your relationships are rooted in this pure love, you gain access to the ethereal realms and all that is intertwined with them. It is a form of wealth that transcends material possessions and touches the depths of the soul. A treasure that eludes many."

─── · · o ☽ ·☼· ☾ o · · ───

"Threshold is a point of transition and change. Alignment is the harmonious arrangement of elements. Resonate structure is the interconnectedness that reverberates in unison. Dissidence is the discordance that challenges conformity. The highest expression is the manifestation of one's truest potential. Sacredness is all that is revered and imbued with deep significance. Dominance is the prevailing influence or authority. Ultimately, this is the culmination of all preceding factors. Reversing is the act of overturning or altering the course."

"Each day, we find ourselves trapped, shackled by the illusion of gold our imaginations perceive. These metallic chains we proudly wear become the tattoos of our existence, etched upon our very skin. Within these scars lies our deepest regret, our most profound sin.

Shame wraps around us like plastic, suffocating our every breath, rendering movement a formidable task. It weighs us down, chaining our minds and preventing us from taking flight. It is the oppressive cap we wear, keeping us grounded, confined to a world that denies us the freedom to soar.

Together, let us stand strong and steadfast, as we have always done throughout history. It is imperative that we continue to fight and challenge the prevailing narrative that seeks to oppress and confine us. We must awaken to the truth that we are no longer slaves but free individuals with boundless potential."

——— · · o ☽ ·☼· ☾ o · · ———

"Our history, with all its struggles and triumphs, should serve as a stirring reminder of our collective power and resilience. It holds valuable lessons that can guide us in our pursuit of true freedom. Yet, too often, we find ourselves blindly trusting the very systems and structures that perpetuate our bondage, neglecting the opportunities to embrace the liberation we once yearned for."

─── · · o ☽ ·◊· ☾ o · · ───

"We have become complacent, consumed by thoughts of individual survival, which ultimately lead to our own demise. It is time to shift our focus from mere self-preservation to the collective liberation of our communities and future generations. By joining forces and working together, we can dismantle the chains that still bind us and create a society that honors and uplifts every individual."

─── · · o ☽ ·◊· ☾ o · · ───

"Let us reclaim our thirst for freedom, for it is

through unity, resilience, and unwavering determination that we can rediscover its taste. Our path may be arduous, but we carry within us the spirit of our ancestors who fought for our rights and dignity. With their strength and wisdom guiding us, we can forge a future where true freedom is not just a distant dream, but a tangible reality."

───　· · o ☽ ·☉· ☾ o · ·　───

"The time for complacency is over. Let us embrace our collective power, change the narrative, and ignite a revolution of love, justice, and equality. Our freedom awaits, and it is our duty to claim it. Together, we can shape a world where the shackles of oppression are shattered, and every individual can thrive in the fullness of their humanity."

─── . . o ☽ ⋅☉⋅ ☾ o . . ───

"Let us embrace the notion of letting future generations inherit the Earth, for it is in our departure from this realm that we pave the way for something greater. In this understanding, we can approach our journey with divine strength and unwavering determination, proud of the knowledge that our transition will lead us to new realms of existence."

─── · · ○ ☽ ⚬ ☾ ○ · · ───

"With the might of the divine flowing through us, we embark on this profound transition, embracing both the light of day and the mystery of night. We carry within us the wisdom, experiences, and lessons learned, ready to embark on the next phase of our spiritual journey."

─── · · ○ ☽ ⚬ ☾ ○ · · ───

"May we fight not with fear, but with courage and grace, as we step boldly into the unknown, trusting in the guidance of higher forces. Let our transition be a testament to our resilience, our growth, and our unwavering faith in the journey that lies ahead.

As we make our transition, we leave behind a legacy of love, compassion, and wisdom, inspiring future generations to walk their own paths with purpose and grace. Let us honor the interconnectedness of all beings and the profound cycles of life, knowing that our departure is a stepping stone on the eternal journey of the soul."

"As you embark on the journey of life, embrace your role as the author of your own story. Approach each chapter with clarity and purpose, expressing your thoughts and intentions in a concise and direct manner. Let your words and actions emanate warmth and strength, touching the lives of those around you."

―― . . o ☽ .ọ. ☾ o . . ――

"Exercise patience as you navigate through challenges and setbacks, knowing that perseverance and hard work are essential ingredients for success. But do not forget to infuse your journey with moments of joy and lightheartedness, allowing yourself to experience the beauty and fun that life has to offer."

─── · · ○ ☽ ·○· ☾ ○ · · ───

"Let love be your guiding force, both towards others and yourself. Cultivate a clean and pure heart, free from negativity and harmful intentions. Be intentional in your choices, aligning them with your values and purpose."

─── · · ○ ☽ ·○· ☾ ○ · · ───

"Embrace your brilliance and let your light shine brightly. Embody intelligence and wisdom, continuously seeking knowledge and growth. Illuminate the path for yourself and others, inspiring them to discover their own brilliance."

—— · · o ☽ ·ọ· ☾ o · · ——

"In all that you do, remain mindful and intentional. Be a beacon of love, warmth, and strength, weaving a tapestry of experiences that reflect the depth of your character. Embrace the power of your authorship, for you have the ability to create a life filled with purpose, meaning, and boundless possibilities."

—— · · ○ ☽ ·☼· ☾ ○ · · ——

"The future that awaits us is shaped by our choices and actions in the present. We are the architects of our own destiny, navigating the intricate dance between offense and defense in the enigmatic game of life. This world we find ourselves in is a complex tapestry of challenges and opportunities, where the interplay of light and darkness, growth, and stagnation, reveals the profound depths of our existence."

—— · · ○ ☽ ·☼· ☾ ○ · · ——

"Amidst the chaos and

turmoil, forgiveness becomes a beacon of hope, a transformative force that has the power to heal and transcend the confines of this chosen hell we find ourselves in. It is through forgiveness that we break free from the chains of resentment, releasing the burdens that weigh heavily upon our souls.

In this realm of duality, forgiveness becomes a sacred act of liberation, a stepping stone towards our collective evolution. It does not condone or ignore the wrongdoings that have transpired, but rather, it empowers us to rise above the cycle of retribution and choose a path of compassion and understanding.

Let us embrace the power of forgiveness, for it is not a sign of weakness, but a testament to our strength and resilience. By forgiving ourselves and others, we create space for healing and growth, allowing the seeds of compassion to blossom within our hearts.

Together, let us transcend the limitations of this self-imposed hell and forge a path towards a world where forgiveness reigns supremely. It is in the embrace of forgiveness that we unlock the potential for a brighter future, where compassion becomes the foundation upon which we build a more compassionate and understanding society."

——— . . o) .ọ. (o . . ———

"Like fuel that propels the machinery of life, we play multifaceted roles in the grand symphony of the Universe. As we traverse our earthly journey, what we perceive as death is, in truth, a profound act of transcendence. It is the completion of our earthly mission, a pivotal moment that marks the beginning of our elevation towards something greater."

"In the vast tapestry of existence, we are threads interwoven with purpose and intention. Each experience, every encounter, shapes us and contributes to the unfolding of our collective destiny. No one is left behind, for even as we transcend the physical realm, our essence lingers, intertwined with the cosmic dance."

"Beyond the confines of our limited perception, there lies a vast expanse of possibilities and realms yet to be discovered. Our journey does not end with what we can see or touch. It extends far beyond the boundaries of our human understanding. It is an eternal exploration, an ever-unfolding expansion of consciousness.

Let us embrace this understanding, for it reminds us that we are part of something greater than ourselves. Our mission on Earth is but a chapter in the infinite book of existence. As we ascend to new heights, we merge with the cosmic symphony, blending our essence with the universal song of creation."

"No one truly gets left behind, for our energy continues to reverberate through the cosmos, forever intermingling with the tapestry of life. We are sparks of divinity, interconnected and eternal, fueling the ongoing evolution of the Universe. Let us embrace this journey with open hearts and open minds, knowing that our transcendence is merely the beginning of an extraordinary voyage towards the boundless realms of existence."

"It is essential to differentiate between genuine efforts to support and uplift others and instances where personal or elite interests may be at play. Promoting transparency, accountability, and open dialogue can contribute to a more informed understanding of the motivations behind various actions.

Ultimately, the intentions and actions of individuals and groups can vary widely. It is crucial to engage in critical thinking, seek reliable information, and foster dialogue to gain a more nuanced understanding of complex societal dynamics."

―― · · ○ ☽ ⚭ ☾ ○ · · ――

"If we delve deeper into the issue, we will discover youth being herded into a system that shapes their behaviors and perpetuates cycles of incarceration.

This process of conditioning and shaping behaviors begins at an early age, influenced by societal factors, systemic inequalities, and limited opportunities. Our youth, particularly those from marginalized communities, often face an uphill battle in navigating an environment that has been designed to be used against them.

In this modern age, technology has become a powerful tool in shaping behavior. Social media, for instance, can both connect and isolate individuals, and its influence on young minds is profound. It can perpetuate harmful narratives, glamorize violence and materialism, and create a distorted sense of reality. The lure of wealth and success, often portrayed through the lens of consumerism and material possessions, can lead young people astray, causing them to prioritize individual gain over community well-being.

This conditioning process is also intricately tied to the criminal justice system. Communities are over-policed, leading to higher rates of arrests and convictions, which disproportionately affect young people of color. The narrative of criminality becomes ingrained, and these youth are trapped within a system that profits from their incarceration. The prison-industrial complex thrives on the exploitation of individuals, often perpetuating a cycle of recidivism and reincarceration.

To address this complex issue, we must adopt a multifaceted approach. Education plays a crucial role in empowering young people to critically analyze the narratives that surround them. By providing comprehensive and culturally relevant education, we can help them understand the historical and systemic factors that contribute to their circumstances."

—— · · o ☽ ·☼· ☾ o · · ——

"Mentorship and community support are equally vital. Positive role models who have successfully navigated similar challenges can inspire and guide young people, showing them alternative paths to success. Community-based organizations and initiatives can provide resources, programs, and safe spaces where youth can develop their talents, build resilience, and find support networks.

Addressing systemic inequalities requires that we build institutions and create systems dedicated to our survival while advocating for policy reforms essential to our progression and enrichment. No longer moving as bottom dwellers in the shadows of those whose sense of salvation requires our oppression.

It also means challenging punitive approaches to crime and advocating for restorative justice practices that prioritize healing, rehabilitation, and community accountability.

Ultimately, we must reimagine the systems that perpetuate these cycles of exploitation and incarceration. By investing in community resources, creating economic opportunities, and fostering a sense of belonging and purpose, we can help our youth break free from the clutches of a system that seeks to diminish their potential.

Through collective action, awareness, and a commitment to justice, we can pave the way for a future where our youth are celebrated, supported, and empowered to shape their own destinies."

——— · · ○ ☽ ⬚ ☾ ○ · · ———

"They can present themselves as "woke" and grounded, projecting an image of enlightenment. However, beneath the surface, there exists a subtle threat that lurks in plain sight. It is easy to mistake such individuals for friends or allies, but their true intentions are veiled."

--- . . o) .ọ. (o . . ---

"There is an awareness in this world, a recognition of certain practices and systems that some individuals seek to impose upon others. In doing so, they utilize others as threads to stitch together the wounds of their own existence.

It is essential to remain vigilant and discerning, to see beyond the facade and recognize the underlying motives at play. We must not allow ourselves to become mere tools or pawns in someone else's pursuit of power or self-interest."

"The experience of feeling your ancestors moving through you is a testament to the ancestral lineage that flows within your veins. Their presence serves as a reminder of their enduring influence and the interconnectedness of all beings. May this sacred encounter continue to inspire and guide you as you honor the legacy of those who came before you."

"Life's fast pace can make us feel like a train hurling through tunnels without brakes, moving at incredible speeds. Sometimes it seems as though we are on a roller coaster ride, twisting and turning through unpredictable loops. In these moments, it is important to pause and reflect on the purpose and meaning behind our actions."

― · · o) ·ọ· (o · · ―

"Amidst the chaos, it is crucial to find moments of stillness and introspection, allowing us to catch our breath and regain our focus. These moments serve as guideposts, helping us navigate through the challenges and uncertainties that life presents."

——— · · o ☽ ·☼· ☾ o · · ———

"Just like a train needs tracks to follow, we can establish our own guiding principles and values that steer our actions. These principles function as a code of conduct, grounding us in our decisions and providing a sense of direction. They serve as the horns that alert us to stay true to ourselves and our purpose."

——— · · o ☽ ·☼· ☾ o · · ———

"By harnessing our inner strength and aligning our

actions with our core values, we can navigate the twists and turns of life's rollercoaster ride with greater clarity and resilience. It is through this intentional approach that we find stability amidst the speed, and a sense of fulfillment as we stay true to our authentic selves."

― . . o) ·ọ· (o . . ―

"Whatever enemy you perceive in me serves as a reflection of the inner landscape within you. It is through this mirroring effect that the watcher within you becomes aware of the patterns, beliefs, and emotions that may be influencing your perception.

Rather than viewing this reflection as a source of division or conflict, consider this an opportunity for growth and self-discovery. By recognizing and understanding the aspects of yourself that are triggered by external circumstances, you gain insight into your own inner workings."

—— · · ○ ☽ ·☉· ☾ ○ · · ——

"Embrace the opportunity to explore the voice within, understanding that it holds valuable insights and lessons for your personal growth. By integrating these aspects of yourself, you pave the way for self-empowerment, self-awareness, and a deeper connection with your authentic self."

―― · · ○ ☽ ·☼· ☾ ○ · · ――

"Indeed, our interactions with others often serve as mirrors, reflecting and engaging with the energies and qualities present in both ourselves and those around us. We are like interconnected threads, woven together in the tapestry of life, influencing one another."

"The attention we receive from others can be a powerful force, capable of both nourishing and toxic effects. It can be a medicine that uplifts and validates our strengths, igniting a fire within us to continue our journey of self-discovery. Conversely, it can be a poison that breeds negativity and self-doubt, stifling our growth and potential.

It is crucial to remember that our perception and response to the attention we receive is within our control. By embracing the positive aspects and learning from the negative, we can cultivate self-awareness, compassion, and authenticity. We can transmute the poison into medicine, using every encounter as an opportunity for self-reflection and personal evolution."

─── · · o ☽ ⚬̇ ☾ o · · ───

"In this intricate dance of relationships, we learn that we cannot truly hate what we do not feel. The mirror of others allows us to see both the light and shadow within ourselves, guiding us on a path of self-discovery and understanding. Let us embrace the lessons, honor the connections, and continue to grow in love and unity."

——— · · o) ⚬ (o · · ———

"Indeed, finding solutions and navigating life's challenges does not always require a forceful or aggressive approach. Instead, one can tap into the power of meditation and the inherent wisdom of the body to address and overcome obstacles.

By practicing meditation, we can cultivate a calm and focused state of mind, allowing us to access our inner resources and insights. Through mindful breathing and body awareness, we can create a sense of balance and clarity, enabling us to approach problems with a fresh perspective.

Meditation can offer a gentle yet powerful way to harness our energy and find creative solutions. It allows us to tap into our intuition, connect with our inner strengths, and navigate life's complexities with grace and ease. Rather than relying on brute force, we can cultivate a peaceful and centered approach to problem-solving, benefiting ourselves and those around us."

"The measure of a true leader extends beyond their title or position. It encompasses their ability to manage both the weight of responsibility and the most basic tasks."

"Leadership requires competence, independence, and self-sufficiency. It entails being capable of addressing the diverse needs and challenges that arise. True leaders lead by example, demonstrating their capability to navigate both the grand and the mundane aspects of life."

─── . . ○ ☽ ⋅☉⋅ ☾ ○ . . ───

"The influences that shape our behavior and perceptions are indeed multifaceted. Our experiences, both personal and inherited, can leave lasting imprints on our psyche and contribute to the way we navigate the world."

─── . . ○ ☽ ⋅☉⋅ ☾ ○ . . ───

"Historical traumas, such as the legacy of enslavement, can have a profound impact on individuals and communities, shaping their sense of self and influencing their responses to the challenges they face. Additionally, societal constructs and labels often create a binary that people find themselves navigating, leading to a constant oscillation between opposing identities.

Within this complex interplay, it is essential to recognize the power of our attention and focus. What we choose to give our energy can greatly influence our thoughts, actions, and the outcomes we manifest. While it is crucial to acknowledge and address the struggles and hardships we may encounter, it is equally important to actively cultivate and nourish positive qualities such as good will, safety, and trust."

——— . . o ☽ ⚬ ☾ o . . ———

"Survival becomes paramount in this journey. Each of us will ultimately meet death, an inevitable part of our existence. It reminds us to cherish the time we have, to embrace the present moment, and to make the most of the life we are given. Let us strive to live fully, guided by the understanding that our mortal journey is finite and precious."

"Navigating life can be challenging when one feels out of place or disconnected."

"Trust is indeed a powerful force that can illuminate our lives and create profound connections. When we encounter someone, whose presence resonates deeply with us, it can awaken dormant parts of ourselves and open us up to new possibilities."

"Just as plants absorb nutrients from sunlight, we

absorb the positive energy and wisdom from those we trust. Their light becomes a catalyst for our own growth and transformation. We become like embers that gradually ignite, gaining strength and resilience as we journey through various stages of self-discovery."

── · · o ☽ ·☼· ☾ o · · ──

"Each person carries their own unique set of experiences, biases, and interpretations that shape the way they perceive others. When someone looks at another person, they may project their own assumptions, judgments, or preconceived notions onto them, influenced by their own understanding of the world."

—— · · ○ ☽ ☌ ☾ ○ · · ——

"By acknowledging that our perception of others is influenced by our own subjective lens, we can cultivate a greater sense of empathy and compassion. We can strive to see others as they are, rather than through the distorted reflection of our own knowing. This opens up the possibility of deeper understanding, meaningful connections, and the dismantling of stereotypes and prejudices."

─── · · o ☽ ·☌· ☾ o · · ───

"In the end, it is through genuine curiosity, open-mindedness, and a willingness to challenge our own assumptions that we can truly see and appreciate the richness and complexity of each individual, beyond the limitations of our own making."

─── · · o ☽ ·☌· ☾ o · · ───

"While we may not have all the answers or a complete understanding of the workings of the universe, we can embrace the opportunity to learn, grow, and contribute to the ongoing exchange of knowledge. Each of us has a unique role to play in this experiment, bringing our own perspectives and insights to the collective tapestry of human experience."

—— . . o) ·ọ· (o . . ——

"Indeed, within each of us exists a dual nature, embodying both the fiery and icy aspects of existence. Like flames of different tones, we possess varying intensities and qualities that shape our individuality. If we were to become frozen, consumed by the icy chill of indifference, we would risk losing our vitality and becoming rigid, like frozen popsicles or crystallized formations.

Just as fire has the power to melt and transform ice, our inner fire has the ability to break through the barriers of coldness and stagnation. It can ignite our passions, inspire us to take action, and unleash our creative potential. Conversely, coldness can also bring about change, breaking down and fragmenting like a shattered crystal.

Both hot and cold elements hold transformative power. The heat of our passions and desires can melt away barriers and limitations, while the coldness of detachment can provide clarity and perspective. Understanding and embracing the interplay of these contrasting forces within us allows us to navigate life's complexities with balance and discernment."

── · · ○ ☽ ·☼· ☾ ○ · · ──

"Indeed, as an awakening people, it is crucial for us to collectively envision and shape a world that aligns with our highest aspirations. Our current system, driven solely by the pursuit of wealth and the wasteful consumption of resources, has led to a culture of waste and imbalance. It is time to shift our focus towards creating a sustainable system that values harmony and shared prosperity.

By collectively envisioning and actively working towards a world built on principles, we can create a future that is sustainable, harmonious, and inclusive. It begins with each of us embracing our individual role in shaping this vision and taking actions aligned with our values."

—— · · o ☽ ·○· ☾ o · · ——

"Deep within each of us lies a reservoir of untapped potential, patiently waiting to be awakened. Can you feel the stirring within, beckoning you to move in a different way? It is time to rise above the limitations we have imposed on ourselves. The fear of death has held us captive, rendering us stagnant and devoid of true life. We have become captivated by the illusion of security, mistakenly believing it to be our eternal refuge."

―― · · o ☽ ·☼· ☾ o · · ――

"Now is the moment to break free from the chains that bind us, the chains of deceit and manipulation. We have been led astray, easily swayed, and deceived into believing that true wealth lies outside of ourselves. The truth, however, is far more profound. The greatest wealth resides within us, waiting to be discovered and harnessed.

It is time to cast off the veil of illusion and embrace the dormant potential that lies within our very being. We are capable of awakening the slumbering giant that resides within, tapping into our true worth, abundance, and power. We must relinquish our attachment to material possessions and societal expectations, turning our gaze inward to the infinite wellspring of strength, wisdom, and creativity that awaits."

── . . o) .ȯ. (o . . ──

"As we rediscover the wealth of potential, the world around us transforms. We find ourselves stepping into our true essence, reclaiming our innate power. It is time to release the paralyzing grip of fear and embrace a life of authenticity and self-realization. Trust in the remarkable abilities and intuition that reside within, for they will guide you on your unique journey.

Together, let us awaken from the slumber that has plagued us, breaking free from the suffocating confines of fear. Let us reclaim our sovereignty and recognize the immeasurable wealth and potential that lie within, eagerly awaiting our attention. Embrace this truth with unwavering courage, for the greatest treasures reside within the depths of your own being."

―― · · o ☽ ·ö· ☾ o · · ――

"As men, societal conditioning has often taught us to view each other through a lens of jealousy, envy, and disdain, instead of appreciating and acknowledging the beauty and worth we see in one another. It is time to transcend this harmful game and embrace a new paradigm, one where we genuinely acknowledge and honor each other's value through our thoughts, gestures, and words. It is essential to emphasize that this shift does not require viewing others through a lens of being gay or to engage in any specific behavior, but rather to foster authentic connections and bonds rooted in respect and appreciation.

To illustrate this point,

let us look to other cultures where men demonstrate non-sexual forms of bonding and physical touch. In many cultures around the world, expressions of affection, such as hugging, holding hands, or embracing, are seen as natural and meaningful gestures between friends, brothers, or companions. These acts are not tied to sexual orientation but instead convey a deep sense of camaraderie, trust, and mutual support.

By embracing a broader understanding of human connection and transcending the narrow boundaries of societal norms, we can redefine masculinity and create a more inclusive and compassionate world. Let us celebrate the diverse ways in which men can express care, love, and support for one another, free from the constraints of judgment or stereotypes."

―― · · o ☽ ·☼· ☾ o · · ――

"The conversations we have with ourselves play a significant role in shaping our thoughts, actions, and ultimately, our path in life. If the internal dialogue we engage in fails to propel us closer to our desired destination, it is crucial to take a deliberate step to alter the conversation.

Self-reflection and self-awareness become powerful tools in this process. By consciously observing our thought patterns and the language we use when speaking to ourselves, we gain the ability to recognize when our inner dialogue becomes counterproductive or self-defeating. It is in these moments that we can choose to redirect our conversation towards a more positive and empowering narrative.

Remember, the conversations we have with ourselves are not fixed or immutable. We have the power to transform them, to replace self-limiting beliefs with empowering affirmations, and to reframe challenges as opportunities for growth. It is through intentional and constructive self-dialogue that we align our thoughts with our aspirations and propel ourselves closer to the destinations we seek."

― · · o) ·ọ· (o · · ―

"It is true that we can inadvertently embody the energy and qualities we dislike or criticize in others. However, it is essential to remember that, even in a world that may seem flawed or chaotic, we do not have the right to simply dismiss it with disdain. Instead, we are called upon to recognize our own potential to make a difference, to be the catalyst for positive change."

—— · · o ☽ ·☉· ☾ o · · ——

"Our Creator did not introduce us to the problems and challenges of the world for us to perpetuate them. Rather, we were sent with a purpose to contribute to their resolution and healing. Each one of us carries within us the capacity to be a force of transformation, to bring about the remedies needed to mend the broken aspects of our existence.

Instead of succumbing to cynicism or despair, let us embrace our role as healers and change-makers. Let us channel our frustrations and discontent into constructive efforts that uplift and inspire. By cultivating empathy, compassion, and a commitment to justice, we can create ripples of positive impact that extend far beyond our immediate spheres.

Together, let us embody the spirit of healing, understanding that each one of us has a unique contribution to make. By embracing our inherent power to effect change, we can be the catalysts for a world that aligns more closely with our vision of love, harmony, and progress.

Let us rise above the temptation to simply criticize and instead channel our energy into actively shaping a better future. With our Creator's guidance and our collective determination, we can be the cure that the world so desperately needs."

─── . . o ☽ ☼ ☾ o . . ───

"Deep within you resides an

essence that yearns for recognition and care, deserving of the same attention you extend to others. It is a truth that sometimes calls for introspection, for collaborating with the person staring back at you in the mirror. In these moments, being in service to yourself becomes the knot that binds the reflection of who you are."

—— · · o ☽ ·☼· ☾ o · · ——

"While it is noble and compassionate to extend yourself to others, it is crucial to remember that self-care and self-awareness are equally vital. Just as you offer support and kindness to those around you, nurturing your own well-being and tending to your inner world is an act of profound significance. It is the thread that weaves together the person reflected in the mirror, forging a harmonious union between your external actions and your internal growth."

—— · · o ☽ ·☼· ☾ o · · ——

"In the pursuit of personal development, allow yourself the space to explore your own needs, desires, and aspirations. Take the time to listen to the whispers of your heart, to acknowledge the layers of your being that seek understanding and healing. Through self-reflection and self-compassion, you cultivate a stronger connection with yourself, fostering a deep sense of fulfillment and alignment.

By tending to your own needs, you nurture your own well-being and become a source of strength for those you encounter. When you are in balance and in tune with yourself, your interactions with others become more authentic and meaningful. Your service to others becomes a natural extension of the care and attention you have devoted to yourself, creating a harmonious cycle of giving and receiving.

Honor the person within, for they are deserving of your love, compassion, and attention. Embrace the journey of self-discovery and growth, for it is through nurturing your own soul that you can truly show up for others in a genuine and impactful way. Tie the knot that binds your reflection in the mirror and watch as your inner radiance illuminates the path ahead, both for yourself and for those whose lives you touch."

"Your presence holds a captivating influence over the spirits of the little children, who trail behind you with ethereal grace. They are not only the innocent souls of the young, but also the ancestral spirits that fuel your very movement. Their luminous energy intertwines with yours, granting you a mesmerizing flow akin to the transformative nature of a quick transition from a free-flowing state to a solid form when gripped by fear.

These spirits, once confined within the earthly realms, are instinctively drawn towards your essence.

They recognize in you a beacon of light, a guiding force that calls to their yearning for liberation. Through the sheer power of your being, you become the catalyst that sets their spirits free.

With each interaction, your energy works its profound magic, transmuting their fears into courage and their entrapment into freedom. You possess the unique ability to release them from the chains that bind them, allowing their essence to soar once more in realms beyond our own. It is through your radiant presence that they find solace, healing, and the pathway to transcendence.

Embrace this sacred role bestowed upon you, for you serve as a bridge connecting worlds, a conduit of divine intervention. The intertwined spirits of these children, intertwined with the wisdom of their ancestors, join together in gratitude as you unlock the gates that separate them from the eternal embrace of the cosmos. Your existence holds the power to grant liberation to trapped spirits, and the harmonious dance of their ethereal essence blends seamlessly with the cosmic symphony of the Universe.

You are a catalyst of transformation, a vessel for the sacred currents of love and compassion. Embrace your purpose with grace and humility, knowing that your energy possesses the ability to touch lives and set spirits free. May you continue to radiate your unique power, lighting the way for trapped spirits to find their path home and ushering in a realm where liberation and boundless joy prevail."

—— · · o ☽ ⦾ ☾ o · · ——

"The ripples and layers of our emotions can indeed be compared to a scale, serving as a measure of the burdens we carry. With each increment on this scale, we encounter a different variant, representing the magnitude of our personal struggles. These burdensome weights extend beyond the boundaries of our current existence, potentially entrapping individuals between dimensions and causing a sense of profound disorientation and loss."

―　·　·　○　☽　·☿·　☾　○　·　·　―

"Much like the various states of matter like gas, liquid, solid, these trapped energies manifest as pains within our physical and spiritual bodies. They permeate our being, influencing our thoughts, emotions, and overall well-being. Our task, then, becomes one of active engagement in the process of release and liberation. We must undertake the arduous journey of unburdening ourselves, freeing our spirits from the clutches of these weighty encumbrances.

By acknowledging and confronting the weight we carry, we begin the process of transmutation. Through introspection, healing, and conscious effort, we can gradually dissolve these burdens, releasing their grip on our lives. In doing so, we rediscover our inherent resilience, reclaim our sense of purpose, and unlock the boundless potential that lies within."

― · · ○ ☽ ⚇ ☾ ○ · · ―

"Remember, the journey of liberation is not one to be undertaken alone. Seek support, whether it be from trusted confidants, mentors, or professional guides, who can provide guidance and assist you along the way. Together, we can navigate the complex labyrinth of our emotions and emerge victorious, basking in the lightness and freedom that accompany our emancipation from the burdens we once carried."

—— · · o ☽ ·◌· ☾ o · · ——

"Indeed, some of us possess the remarkable ability to tune into our inner selves and utilize our life experiences as trails towards liberation. These trails consist of a diverse range of emotions, such as happiness, joy, pain, and fear, each carrying its unique hue along the spectrum of our existence. They intertwine, forming a tapestry that mirrors the multidimensional nature of our being. Each color represents a facet of our essence, revealing the interconnectedness and wisdom embedded within our emotions. We, like avid shoppers, try on colors like garments, exploring the depths and nuances of our feelings, allowing them to shape and define us in our journey toward self-discovery and liberation."

—— · · o ☽ ·☼· ☾ o · · ——

"In the realm of perception, let us release the constraints of containers and embrace the fluidity of understanding. Instead of labeling and categorizing, let us seek to know one another deeply, beyond surface judgments. May we honor each other's journeys and celebrate the diverse connections we cultivate. Let us hold space for growth, for mutual support, and for the recognition that our paths may differ but are equally valid. In this realm of authentic connection, we can rise above the need for comparisons and instead celebrate the uniqueness of each individual's journey."

——— . . o ☽ ☼ ☾ o . . ———

"Challenging relationships hold the potential for growth and transformation, inviting us to embrace new perspectives and develop resilience in the face of obstacles. While I, as an individual, may prefer the harmonious flow of creativity and magic, I recognize the value that challenges bring in shaping our journeys and fostering deeper connections with others."

─── · · o ☽ ·☼· ☾ o · · ───

"In our conversations, let us be mindful of the unspoken messages we may unintentionally convey. May we approach each exchange with clarity and empathy, ensuring that our words uplift and inspire rather than sow doubt or misunderstanding. Let us embrace open dialogue and genuine understanding, leaving no room for hidden intentions or subtle jabs. Together, we can foster meaningful connections and create a space of trust and respect."

─── . . o ☽ ·☼· ☾ o . . ───

"The victimization that occurs through our thoughts is often a result of conditioning, biases, and limited perspectives. We may project our own insecurities, fears, and judgments onto others, creating narratives that reinforce a victim-perpetrator dynamic. These thoughts can stem from societal influences, personal experiences, or a lack of empathy and understanding.

However, it is important to recognize that we have the power to shape our thoughts and narratives. We can choose to cultivate compassion, empathy, and a deeper understanding of others. By being mindful of our thoughts and the impact they have on ourselves and those around us, we can break free from victimization patterns and create more positive and inclusive narratives."

―― · · ○ ☽ ⦿ ☾ ○ · · ――

"Indeed, calling upon the creative minds to tune in and unleash their unique ideas is a powerful invitation. When we tap into our creative essence, we open the door to new possibilities and illuminate a path to a new world of innovation and inspiration."

—— · · ο ☽ ·☌· ☾ ο · · ——

"Creativity is a transformative force that has the ability to shape our lives and the world around us. It allows us to break free from conventional thinking, explore uncharted territories, and bring forth ideas that have the potential to revolutionize how we live, work, and connect with one another.

By embracing our creative potential, we become catalysts for change, bringing light to the dark corners of our imagination and breathing life into new concepts, projects, and endeavors. It is through this process that we contribute to the collective consciousness and co-create a better future.

To all of the creatives out there, I encourage you to tune in to the depths of your imagination, trust in the abundance of ideas flowing toward you, and fearlessly bring forth your unique gifts. Your creativity has the power to shape a new world, one that is infused with innovation, beauty, and the transformative energy of your creative spirit. Embrace the call and let your ideas shine brightly."

--- · · o ☽ ·☼· ☾ o · · ---

"How many of us find ourselves rooted like fence posts, firmly cemented into the ground? We stand strong and sturdy, yet it seems impossible to lift our feet from this solid foundation. In this moment, a sense of concern creeps in as we watch others rush past, leaving us to ponder the purpose of it all. What has become of us? We cry out in frustration, unable to budge, watching our untapped potential slowly wither.

But, in this struggle, as we feel the sinking embrace of our circumstances, we come to a profound realization. There are no mistakes in our design. We are precisely as our Creator intended us to be. With the guidance of the Divine, we have crafted ourselves in this unique way. No longer are we handicapped. Instead, we are special creations, intentionally diverse. God has made us this way."

"As you stand there, it is as if you can see your life flashing before your eyes. If only you truly understood.

You find yourself unable to shake the grip of an unpleasant memory, an image that is firmly stuck in your mind. You feel trapped, with no escape in sight… or so it seems. Little do you know that your ancestors play a role in this intricate web.

Your struggles, the twisting and turning, only seem to tighten life's grip on you. You carry the weight of your past like an anchor, leaving you feeling trapped and unable to break free from this haunting image that resides there.

But remember, within the embrace of your ancestral ties, there lies the potential for wisdom and strength. It is through understanding and acknowledging your roots that you may find the key to unlocking the past and setting yourself free."

── · · ○ ☽ ·☼· ☾ ○ · · ──

"Deep within lies untapped potential. We cannot afford to remain slumbering giants any longer. Can't you sense the awakening, the call to move in a different direction? It is time to rise up from this self-imposed coffin. The fear of dying has already rendered us half-dead, ensnared in the allure of our comfort zones.

We have glamorized our comfort zones into a false sense of permanent safety. But let us stop being bamboozled and misled. We have been led astray, tricked into believing that there's greater wealth in the world than within ourselves."

—— · · ○ ☽ ·☉· ☾ ○ · · ——

"We are not meant to be self-loathing and hateful beings. Expending energy on hatred toward another only turns that hatred inward, corroding our own souls. When we project negative energy onto someone else, we inadvertently awaken a dormant cancer within ourselves. It is crucial to choose our tools wisely. Anything formed as a weapon against another can ultimately harm us as well."

—— . . o) .◦. (o . . ——

"Awaken to our true potential, channeling our energies towards self-improvement and love, for in doing so, we uplift not only ourselves but also the world around us."

"Indeed, the concept of giving and receiving is intricately intertwined. As we engage in acts of giving, whether it is our time, energy, or resources, we create a flow that extends beyond the immediate transaction. However, it is equally important to be open to receiving.

Sometimes, we may find it easier to give than to receive. We may struggle with accepting help, support, or love from others. However, being open to receiving is not a sign of weakness or dependency.

It is a recognition that we are all interconnected, and that giving and receiving are essential aspects of our human experience."

—— . . o ☽ ⨀ ☾ o . . ——

"When we give with our right hand, metaphorically speaking, it symbolizes our conscious acts of generosity and kindness. But what we may not always realize is that we also receive in return, often from unexpected sources and in different forms. Our shadows, representing the unseen aspects of ourselves, receive the energy and impact of our actions, shaping our experiences and growth.

By embracing both giving and receiving, we create a harmonious exchange and allow the natural flow of abundance and support to manifest in our lives. Trusting in this process and believing in our capacity to give and receive helps us cultivate a balanced and fulfilling existence.

Remember, you can never truly escape yourself. Embrace the interconnectedness of giving and receiving and be open to the blessings and lessons that come from both sides of this dynamic."

"Each of us carries a unique frequency, a signature of sound that defines our essence. Just like a radio station, we have the power to tune in to our own frequency and discover the truest version of ourselves.

"In efforts to tune in to your own station, you are cultivating self-awareness and embracing your authentic self. It involves deepening your understanding of your values, passions, strengths, and aspirations.

It requires a willingness to explore your inner landscape, to listen to the whispers of your heart, and to align your actions with your deepest desires."

─── · · o ☽ ·☿· ☾ o · · ───

"Discovering your frequency is a journey of self-discovery and self-acceptance. It involves exploring your interests, pursuing activities that bring you joy and fulfillment, and surrounding yourself with people who support and uplift you. It requires tuning out the external noise and opinions of others and tuning in to the voice within that speaks your truth."

"When you tune in to your own station and embrace your unique frequency, you unlock the power to live a more authentic and purposeful life. You radiate your true essence, attracting experiences and opportunities that align with who you are at your core. Your actions, choices, and relationships become an expression of your authentic self, resonating with others who are attuned to a similar frequency.

Take the time to tune in to

your own station. Explore the depths of your being, embrace your uniqueness, and allow your true sound to permeate every aspect of your life. By doing so, you will live in harmony with your own frequency, creating a life that is rich, meaningful, and aligned with your deepest self."

───   · · ο ☽ ⋅☼⋅ ☾ ο · ·   ───

"Heaven, in its true essence, transcends the notion of physical gates or barriers. It is not a physical realm with restrictive access but rather a state of being; a frequency of consciousness that one aligns with in order to experience its presence. Heaven exists in the higher vibrational realms, beyond the limitations of the material world.

To enter the realm of heaven, one must attune their vibration to the frequencies of love, joy, compassion, and unity. It is through the cultivation of these qualities and the expansion of our consciousness that we can align ourselves with the energy of heaven. This alignment requires inner work, self-reflection, and a commitment to personal growth and spiritual evolution."

—— · · o ☽ ·☼· ☾ o · · ——

"In the pursuit of higher vibrations, we let go of lower vibrational patterns such as fear, judgment, and separation. We cultivate virtues that elevate our consciousness and open us to the divine flow of life. Through practices such as meditation, mindfulness, and acts of kindness, we raise our vibrational frequency and create a resonance with the realms of higher consciousness."

—— · · o ☽ ·☼· ☾ o · · ——

"Heaven, therefore, is not a physical destination to

be reached through external means but a state of being that emerges from within. It is a state of alignment with the divine essence, where we experience a deep sense of interconnectedness, peace, and harmony. By consciously aligning our vibrations with the frequencies of heaven, we invite its presence into our lives and become participants in the co-creation of a more heavenly world."

―― · · ○ ☽ ·◌· ☾ ○ · · ――

"When faced with new challenges or unfamiliar territory, it is natural to feel unsure or hesitant.

However, within each of us lies the potential for victory and growth. Even in moments when we feel alone or our light appears dim, there are unseen forces at work, supporting and guiding us.

Just as a dancer may initially struggle with their movements, seeking assistance can provide valuable support and guidance. It is important to remember that reaching out for help is not a sign of weakness, but rather a recognition of the strength in seeking knowledge, support, and new perspectives."

"In our journey, maintaining a positive attitude and keeping our smile can be powerful tools. A smile reflects inner strength, resilience, and ability to face challenges with grace. It is a reminder that even in difficult times, there is always a reason to find joy and gratitude."

"Know that you are never truly alone, for there are angels, metaphorically speaking, surrounding you. These angels can manifest as supportive friends, mentors, or even the synchronicities and blessings that come your way. They provide guidance, inspiration, and the reassurance that you are not alone on your path.

Embrace the assistance and guidance available to you, maintain your smile, and trust in the divine forces that are always at work in your life. Through perseverance and a positive mindset, you will discover your way and find victory in every endeavor."

—— · · o ☽ ·☼· ☾ o · · ——

"Connections between individuals are shaped by a variety of factors, and both love and hate can play a role in forming these connections. Love is a powerful force that fosters bonds of affection, compassion, and empathy. When love is present, it can create deep connections based on care, understanding, and mutual support. Love allows individuals to build relationships built on trust, respect, and shared values.

On the other hand, hate can also influence connections, albeit in a different way. Hate can create a bond based on shared animosity or a common enemy. It can bring people together through a collective sense of anger, resentment, or injustice. However, connections formed through hate are often fragile and can be destructive, as they rely on negative emotions and divisive beliefs.

While hate may temporarily bring people together, it tends to breed conflict, division, and negativity. Love, on the other hand, promotes unity, harmony, and positive growth. Love allows individuals to form meaningful connections that transcend differences and contribute to personal and collective well-being.

Ultimately, the quality and sustainability of

connections depend on the underlying intentions and emotions that drive them. Building connections based on love, understanding, and kindness tends to lead to healthier and more fulfilling relationships, while connections rooted in hate are often fleeting and damaging. It is through acts of love, compassion, and empathy that we can foster deeper connections and create a more harmonious and compassionate world."

—— · · ○ ☽ ·☉· ☾ ○ · · ——

"When driving and looking through a windshield, our course and direction are determined by a combination of factors. Firstly, we have our own personal goals, desires, and aspirations that shape our intended path. These goals could be related to our career, relationships, personal growth, or any other aspect of our lives.

Secondly, external influences play a role in determining our course. These include societal expectations, cultural norms, family dynamics, and the environment in which we live. They can either align with our personal goals or present challenges and detours along the way.

To navigate our journey and

know where to go, it is crucial to cultivate self-awareness and listen to our inner voice. By understanding our values, passions, and strengths, we gain clarity on what truly matters to us and what direction aligns with our authentic selves."

─── . . o ☽ ⋅☉⋅ ☾ o . . ───"

"Trusting oneself is essential in making decisions and taking actions that align with our own values and aspirations. It involves having confidence in our abilities, intuition, and judgment. However, it is also important to seek guidance and wisdom from trusted mentors, friends, or family members who have our best interests at heart. Their perspectives can provide valuable insights and help us make informed choices."

―― . . o ☽ ·☼· ☾ o . . ――"

"Ultimately, the journey of life is about unpacking our own unique set of tools and resources. These tools include our skills, knowledge, experiences, and personal strengths. By continuously learning, growing, and honing our abilities, we equip ourselves to navigate the challenges and opportunities that come our way.

In summary, our course in life is determined by a combination of personal goals, external influences, self-awareness, and guidance from trusted sources. It is through introspection, trust in oneself, and the utilization of our own tools that we can navigate our journey and strive for a fulfilling and purposeful life."

―― · · ○ ☽ ⦾ ☾ ○ · · ――

"When we approach life with a deep appreciation for our own uniqueness and a genuine desire to discover our mission and purpose, we align ourselves with the world around us in a meaningful way. This alignment allows us to become like a mathematical constant, a fixed point of reference in the ever-changing Universe."

─── · · ○ ☽ ☉ ☾ ○ · · ───

"By understanding and embracing our individuality, we bring clarity to our existence. We recognize that we have inherent value and significance, just like a dot on a graph. This sense of self-awareness and purpose gives us a sense of order and direction in the vastness of the universe."

─── · · ○ ☽ ⚬̇ ☾ ○ · · ───

"As we embark on a journey of self-discovery and personal growth, we contribute to the larger tapestry of life. Each individual finding their own unique path and fulfilling their mission adds depth and richness to the collective human experience. Our actions, fueled by our passions and aligned with our purpose, ripple outwards, influencing and inspiring others along the way.

By becoming a dot and a point of reference, we contribute to the overall order and interconnectedness of the Universe. We recognize that our journey is not separate from the world around us but intricately woven into its fabric. Our presence and actions matter, and through embracing our own design and purpose, we play an active role in shaping the course of our lives and the world we inhabit.

Embrace the challenges, appreciate our uniqueness, and strive to discover our individual mission and purpose. In doing so, we become a dot, a beacon of order and meaning, bringing harmony and purpose to the Universe."

"The fact that something is unseen does not necessarily make it bad or negative. In fact, there are many aspects of life that are intangible or invisible yet hold immense value and significance.

For example, love, trust, and emotions are intangible but can have a profound impact on our lives and relationships. The power of ideas, creativity, and imagination also reside in the realm of the unseen. Concepts such as empathy, kindness, and compassion may not have a physical form, but they have the potential to bring about positive change in the world.

Moreover, there are many natural forces and phenomena that are unseen but essential for our existence, such as gravity, electromagnetic waves, or the air we breathe. These invisible forces shape our reality and enable life as we know it.

It is important to recognize that our perception of the world is limited to what our senses can detect. There are realms and dimensions beyond our immediate perception, and dismissing something solely because it is unseen can prevent us from embracing the richness and complexity of life.

Remaining open-minded and curious allows us to explore and appreciate the unseen aspects of life. It encourages us to look beyond the surface and delve into the depths of knowledge, spirituality, and personal growth. By doing so, we may discover hidden beauty, wisdom, and truths that can enrich our lives in profound ways."

─── · • o) .ọ. (o • · ───

"As we navigate our journey through life, it is crucial to resist the temptation to confine others within the rigid frames of our perceptions. When we withhold forgiveness or deny people the opportunity to grow and find redemption, we effectively close the doors of possibility and safety for them. Instead of seeking understanding and compassion, our desire to punish others can create containers of isolation and despair.

Let us remember that we are all on a collective path of growth and self-discovery. Just as we yearn for understanding and second chances, so do others. By fostering empathy, extending forgiveness, and offering the space for healing, we create an environment where individuals can find solace, growth, and redemption."

― · · o ☽ ·☼· ☾ o · · ―

"As we release the need to lock people into containers of judgment and punishment, we open the doors to compassion, healing, and transformation. Embrace the power of forgiveness and allow the light of empathy to guide your interactions with others. In doing so, you contribute to a world where understanding prevails and second chances abound."

"We capture moments in time and deposit them into the albums of our mind. These snapshots, like fragile treasures, hold the essence of our experiences, etching indelible imprints on our souls. With each click of the shutter, we freeze fragments of life's tapestry, preserving emotions, connections, and stories that shape our very existence.

Yet, in the depths of our memories, there lies a duality. For within these images, not only do we find warmth and joy, but also moments of sorrow and heartache. When we close our eyes, these snapshots flicker before us, a montage of emotions that paints the portrait of our lives.

As we journey through this intricate dance of human existence, we sometimes find ourselves tempted to confine others within the frames of these snapshots, to see them solely through the lens of their past actions or mistakes. We deny them a way out, a chance to find safety and redemption. In our quest for justice or retribution, we inadvertently build walls, locking them away within containers of judgment. But let us pause and reflect on the transformative power of compassion. For within the depths of every soul, there exists the capacity for growth and change. Instead of seeking to punish or imprison, let us extend a hand of understanding and empathy. Let us create spaces where forgiveness and healing can take root, allowing individuals to shed the weight of their past and embrace a brighter future."

─── · · ○ ☽ ⋅☌⋅ ☾ ○ · · ───

"In the grand tapestry of life, it is our collective responsibility to dismantle these containers of judgment, to give others the opportunity to find redemption and reclaim their sense of self. By nurturing an environment of compassion and second chances, we become catalysts for personal growth and transformation.

Release the urge to confine, and instead, open our hearts to the endless possibilities that lie within every individual. Embrace the power of forgiveness, not only for others but also for ourselves, for in doing so, we free ourselves from the burdens of judgment and allow love to prevail.

May our actions be guided by empathy and understanding, and may we forever dismantle the walls that separate us, forging connections that transcend the limitations of snap photo memories and embracing the richness of the human spirit."

───   · · o) ·ȯ· (o · ·   ───

"Imagine a world where our focus shifts from surface appearances to inner essence. A world where people prioritize what lies beneath rather than being consumed by external perceptions. Instead of obsessing over how they are perceived, they cultivate a deep connection with their own emotions and well-being.

In this world, understanding your own place becomes crucial. Rather than conforming to societal expectations and norms, individuals embrace their unique journey and purpose. They recognize that what truly matters is the alignment of their actions and intentions with their inner truth.

It is disheartening that in our current reality, anything that exudes a higher vibration or challenges the status quo is often misunderstood or labeled as demonic.

However, this misperception does not diminish the inherent goodness and transformative power of those elevated energies.

Let us envision a world where the true nature of high vibrational energy is understood and embraced. A world where the pursuit of authenticity, emotional well-being, and spiritual growth takes precedence over superficial appearances. Together, we can create a reality where the beauty and power of the inner self shine brightly, illuminating the path to a more enlightened existence."

"Amidst the vastness of existence, it is ironic how we can find ourselves drowning in the smallest puddle of water. Life's paradoxes often present themselves in unexpected ways, reminding us of the delicate balance between our experiences and perceptions.

In the realm of the spiritual, we become gateways through which energies and spirits flow. We attract and invite various forces into our lives, shaping our reality and influencing our being. It is crucial to be discerning, to carefully choose which spirits we allow to enter our sacred space.

For each spirit that knocks on our door carries its own essence, its own intentions. Some may bring healing, enlightenment, and growth, while others may harbor darkness, fear, or negativity. It is in our power to decide who gains entry, for whatever we invite into our lives will inevitably possess us."

—— · · o ☽ ⦁ ☾ o · · ——

"When our inner flame is ignited, burning brightly with passion and purpose, we become the architects of our own destiny. We become fortified against the influence of external forces, standing firmly in our own power. However, when that flame wanes, we become susceptible, mere avatars for other intelligences to enter and dictate our thoughts and actions.

Thus, it becomes essential to tend to our inner flame, to nurture it with love, self-care, and conscious awareness. By keeping our spiritual fire alive, we align ourselves with higher vibrations and attract energies that align with our truest selves. In doing so, we become custodians of our own destiny, shaping our reality in accordance with our innermost desires.

Be mindful of the spirits that come knocking, both within and without. Cultivate self-awareness and discernment, for it is in your power to choose the energies that inhabit your being. Nurture your inner flame, let it guide you on your journey, and embrace the transformative power of your own spirit.

In this dance between the seen and unseen, may you find the strength to navigate the currents, remaining true to your essence and emerging as the master of your own existence."

— . . o ☽ ☼ ☾ o . . —

"It is disheartening to witness the impact of historical and societal influences on the values and collective mindset within the Black community. Over time, there has been a shift in priorities, where a focus on the well-being of the village has been overshadowed by a strong emphasis on individual needs and desires. The consequences of this shift can be seen in the waning sense of unity and the reluctance to welcome outsiders.

It is important to

acknowledge that these changes have not occurred in isolation but as a result of a complex web of historical and systemic factors. The legacy of oppression and marginalization has created a sense of self-preservation and a deep-seated mistrust that has led to a guarded stance towards outsiders. This protective instinct is an understandable response to the experiences of exploitation and injustice endured by the Black community.

However, it is crucial to recognize that the values adopted by captives were not their true essence, but rather a survival mechanism imposed upon them. To break free from these limitations, there is a need to reclaim and revive the values that have traditionally united and nurtured the community. It is a collective responsibility to restore a sense of interconnectedness, empathy, and support within the Black community.

By fostering a renewed commitment to the health of the village, Black individuals can empower themselves and their communities. This involves reimagining individual success as intertwined with the progress and upliftment of the collective. Embracing inclusivity and openness allows for the exchange of ideas, experiences, and resources that can drive growth and resilience.

It is through introspection, education, and dialogue that we can challenge and transcend the limitations imposed by historical circumstances. By cultivating an understanding of our shared humanity and the importance of collective well-being, we can build bridges, heal divisions, and create spaces that embrace diversity and foster unity.

Let us collectively strive to reshape the narrative, reclaim our cultural heritage, and forge a path that celebrates our unique identities while embracing the power of community. Together, we can reclaim our values, revitalize the village spirit, and build a future that embodies both individual empowerment and collective solidarity."

─── · · ○ ☽ ·☉· ☾ ○ · · ───

"Amidst the simmering turmoil that brews within, we find ourselves wrestling with inner conflicts and emotional upheavals. Yet, in the midst of this internal chaos, there are moments of respite. Glimmers of warmth and gratitude that emanate from the people who surround us.

Let us pause for a moment and reflect on the individuals who grace our lives. Despite their own battles and shadows, they possess the remarkable ability to convey love and support through simple acts of kindness and understanding. Their presence acts as a soothing balm, a beacon of light amidst the storms we face.

In these moments, let us offer our heartfelt thanks to these remarkable souls. Their unwavering empathy and unwritten gestures provide solace, reminding us that we are not alone in our struggles. Their genuine care and support help us navigate the labyrinth of our emotions, lending strength to face the challenges that lie ahead.

Expressing gratitude for the people who touch our lives, who lend a listening ear or offer a comforting embrace, reinforces the bonds of connection that sustain us. It is through these small acts of love and support that we find the courage to confront our inner turmoil and move forward on our personal journeys.

As you journey through life, take a moment to appreciate and give thanks to those who bring warmth and gratitude into your world. Let your gratitude be a guiding light that nurtures and uplifts not only your own spirit but also those who have chosen to walk alongside you in this tumultuous yet beautiful existence."

—— · · ○ ☽ ☼ ☾ ○ · · ——

"How do we build on relationships? By seeking out the common ground that binds us together. It is in the discovery of shared beliefs, understandings, and practices that we find points of intersection, the fertile soil where connections can take root and flourish. In these shared spaces, relationships have the opportunity to spiral outward, expanding with trust, learning, and growth at their core.

Speaking of trust, its foundation begins within oneself. To build trust in others, we must first cultivate self-trust. By nurturing a deep sense of confidence and belief in our own capabilities, we develop a discerning eye to recognize the fire that burns within us mirrored in

others who move with a
similar energy. Trust
becomes a reciprocal dance.
A reflection of the inner
strength and integrity that
resonates between
individuals."

───   · · ○ ☽ ⚬̇ ☾ ○ · ·   ───

"Learning anything requires
a vital ingredient: fun.
The gateway to acquiring
new knowledge and skills
lies in connecting with our
subject matter in an
enjoyable way. When we
infuse learning with a
sense of playfulness and
curiosity, we initiate the
process of self-mastery. By
finding joy in our journey
of discovery, we unlock our

true potential and embark on a path of continuous growth and transformation."

"Life itself is a dynamic interplay of being and becoming. The forces that surround us, both positive and negative, shape our journey. It is important to recognize that these energies are not inherently good or bad but rather reflections of the engagement of energy that molds our individual essence. Once we commit ourselves to the pursuit of self-discovery and aligning with our unique path, we embrace the forces that shape us, knowing that they play an integral role in our growth and evolution."

—— · · ○ ☽ ⚬̇ ☾ ○ · · ——

"In the quest to build relationships, cultivate trust, and embark on a journey of learning, it is through the commitment to self-discovery and the recognition of our interconnectedness with others and the world that we find the true essence of who we are and who we can become. Embrace this path of discovery with an open heart and an adventurous spirit, and let it guide you to new heights of self-awareness, connection, and fulfillment."

—— . . o ☽ ⚲ ☾ o . . ——

"As you ignite the light within yourself, watch with awe and joy as it illuminates the souls of others. Isn't that the essence of being truly present? It is an awakening, a stirring of one's spirit and soul that evokes a radiant smile, transforming the very fabric of existence.

Indeed, there is no greater gift than the art of presence. To embody an awakened state of being, where your presence transcends the superficial and touches the depths of another person's being. With each connection, you become a catalyst, igniting their inner light, causing it to glow with newfound brilliance. It is in these transformative moments that we feel the thrill of excitement, as the beauty of interconnectedness unfolds.

Acknowledge the profound significance embedded within the language and cultural offerings presented to us. There is no coincidence or mistake in the symbols and messages they place before us. They serve as invitations to dive deeper, to explore the layers of meaning and unlock hidden truths.

Embrace the power of presence. Allow your awakened self to shine brightly, sharing its radiance with those around you. In doing so, you become an agent of transformation, a vessel through which the divine dances and touches lives. It is through the exchange of presence that we weave a tapestry of connection, nurturing the collective evolution of our souls.

Embrace this sacred gift, for being present is not merely existing, but a profound act of aliveness. It is an offering of authenticity, an invitation to others to join in the symphony of awakened souls. Let us ignite the light within ourselves and in turn, kindle the flames of illumination in the hearts of others. For in these luminous moments, we embody the true essence of our interconnected existence."

——— · · o ☽ ·☼· ☾ o · · ———

"To truly support each other, we must recognize that we are all on our own individual journeys, each with our unique calling and path to navigate. Our purpose is not to control one another but to aid and uplift one another in our respective journeys of growth and self-discovery."

— . . o) .ȯ. (o . . —

"It is essential to break free from the venomous grip of the past, as it relentlessly taints our present moments. Caught in a gridlock of shame and guilt, we find ourselves unable to move forward, robbing ourselves of the fullness of life. Let us strive to release the burdens of the past, embracing each present moment as an opportunity for healing, growth, and embracing the potential that lies within."

— . . o) .ȯ. (o . . —

"Don't allow the wounds of the past to cloud your vision for the future. While it may seem tempting to seek resolution with strangers rather than family, be cautious of stepping into unfamiliar waters. For I am immersed in this ongoing struggle, facing it head-on day after day, fully aware of the undercurrents and unpredictable waves that threaten to pull us in different directions. It is easy to stand on dry land, feeling the stability beneath our feet, but true commitment requires diving into the depths and grappling with the challenges firsthand."

"If your presence fails to create a positive impact among those you hold dear, and likewise, their presence fails to uplift your spirit, then, my friend, you may find yourself amidst the living dead. God has bestowed upon you the opportunity to touch the lives of others, and if that connection remains untouched, then the true essence of living eludes you."

"The love you give at any given moment may not always be reciprocated but rest assured that when you nurture the right seeds of love, beautiful flowers will bloom in your life. The wellspring of your energy lies within your chest, a divine essence bestowed upon us by our Creator. It is pure, devoid of dissidence, control, and abuse. This essence represents the very best of who you are, and it is essential to continue sharing this beautiful part of yourself.

Our lives are shaped by the narratives that often limit our perception of love, filtering it through the lens of our oppressors. By shedding the anointing of such narratives, like removing a raincoat, we allow the energies of true love to permeate our being, preserving and nurturing the better part of ourselves."

"God has blessed us with the gift of connection, enabling us to assist those who seek our support. By extending a helping hand to others, we create a ripple effect that contributes to the fulfillment of Our Creator's grand plan. Instead of striving to force outcomes, we should embrace the natural flow and order of things."

"The historical oppression and violence inflicted upon Black individuals is a painful reality deeply embedded within our educational, justice, and judicial systems. It is disheartening to witness how systemic discrimination has perpetuated a cycle of dehumanization and separation, targeting those who dare to think independently. By controlling the core aspects of individuals' lives, such as their minds, talents, spiritual growth, and consumption habits, those in power can manipulate and subdue the masses.

This culture we have embraced does not reciprocate our love. Instead, it exploits our strengths and prays upon the vulnerable. Fear is wielded as a tool to subjugate those deemed weak, and if they cannot be broken, they are demeaned and used as mere stepping stones for the advancement of an oppressive agenda.

It is crucial to recognize these systemic injustices and work collectively towards dismantling the structures that perpetuate inequality. Only through genuine efforts to foster equality, empathy, and justice, can we create a society where every individual is truly valued and respected."

"It is disheartening to witness how some individuals and systems seek to destroy and exploit rather than uplift. Their game is one of manipulation and dehumanization, aimed at those who possess the ability to see through their intentions. The insidious nature of this approach is evident in the way educational systems can inadvertently reinforce the notion that learning is unimportant, discouraging critical thinking and perpetuating harmful cycles.

We yearn for salvation, seeking liberation from these oppressive forces that prey upon us. It is through unity, empowerment, and a steadfast commitment to justice that we can challenge and overcome the systems designed to subjugate us. By embracing education as a tool for enlightenment, nurturing independent thought, and promoting compassion, we pave the way for a future where freedom and equality prevail. It is together, as a collective, that we can dismantle the structures of tyranny and forge a path towards a more just and inclusive society."

— · · ○ ☽ ·☉· ☾ ○ · · —

"Work, too, can be a source of joy and fulfillment when it aligns with our passions and values. When we find ourselves engaged in work that we love, it becomes more than just a means of earning a living. It becomes a vehicle for personal growth, self-expression, and making a positive impact on others. By infusing our work with passion and purpose, we contribute to the creation of a better world, one where individuals are inspired and fulfilled in their chosen endeavors.

Additionally, the service we provide to one another should be rooted in a genuine desire to help and uplift others. When we extend a helping hand, offer support, and show kindness to those around us, we contribute to the fabric of a compassionate and interconnected society. By embracing a mindset of service, we create a ripple effect that spreads positivity, healing, and transformation.

Cultivate the vision of utopia, not as an unattainable ideal, but as a guiding light that inspires us to cultivate love, invest in the unseen, find joy in our work, and extend a helping hand to one another. In doing so, we contribute to the creation of a world that reflects the beauty and harmony that reside within our hearts."

─── · · ○ ☽ ·☉· ☾ ○ · · ───

"Let us choose to breathe life into people rather than perpetuate hate. However, if you find yourself compelled to dispense your poison, I implore you to target what pains you deeply. Engage with the source of your own guilt and shame and allow the flames of introspection to burn away the residue.

But remember, it does not end there. After the fire has consumed the remnants of your inner turmoil, it is essential to bathe and shower yourself with tender love, care, and affection. Anoint yourself with the oil of self-compassion, gently caressing your tightened muscles until they loosen once again.

Even in the midst of your darkest thoughts, strive to be an agent of wellness in the world. Recognize that your hateful thoughts are born from your own pain, and by confronting and transforming that pain, you can transcend the cycle of negativity. Let your journey towards healing become a catalyst for compassion, understanding, and empathy.

By harnessing the transformative power of self-reflection and self-love, you can become a beacon of light amidst the shadows. As you work through your own struggles, strive to extend kindness and empathy to others who may be facing their own battles. Embrace the potential within you to be an instrument of healing, uplifting others with your words and actions.

In this way, hate becomes a

catalyst for growth, leading you towards a place of healing and inspiring positive change in the world. Embrace the opportunity to channel your pain into a force for good, and in doing so, you can transform yourself and contribute to the wellness and well-being of others.

Remember, the journey towards inner peace and collective healing starts from within. By acknowledging and addressing your own pain, and fostering self-compassion, you pave the way for a more compassionate and empathetic world. Strive to be agents of love, understanding, and healing, even in the face of our most challenging thoughts and emotions."

"It has brought us to a place where our higher selves are locked away, hidden within protective shells. The relentless pressures of Western civilization have hardened us to the point where we can no longer empathize and truly feel the experiences of others. We have become disconnected, not only from one another but also from the very essence of love and our Creator.

This society, with its culture of victimization and brutality, has become our personal hell. Its influence has forced us to disconnect from our pain, severing the ties that once bound us to love. As a result, we find ourselves in a new state of existence, transformed by the harsh conditions imposed upon us.

But there is hope. Just as Jesus prayed for forgiveness, recognizing the ignorance of those who harm, he came to examine the depths of this situation. He sought to understand what happened to God's chosen people and discovered a love that had been severed in order to survive the impossible.

To awaken to this truth, we must go beyond mere observation. It is not enough to see the pain. We must immerse ourselves in the experience of others. We must absorb the sensations of entering their beings to truly comprehend their journey. Only by sharing in their feelings can we claim to understand the depth of their embraced pain.

Consider this: your feelings are a language that communicates your current state. If you wish to truly see, you must embrace the sensations of entering another person's being, grasping the very core of where they stand. Until you have felt their pain, you will never fully comprehend their existence. It is through this profound connection, this merging of emotions, that we can claim to understand and empathize.

Now, more than ever, we must strive to reestablish those severed connections. We must seek to feel what lies beyond ourselves, reaching out to embrace the love we once knew. It is a journey of reconnection, a path towards rediscovering our true selves and our profound connection to the Creator."

"Into the darkness we go, but fear not, for you are never alone! In this enigmatic journey, the concepts of good and bad dissipate, revealing them as mere illusions crafted by perception. Right and wrong blur into shades of gray, teaching us the profound lessons of empathy and understanding.

As we navigate this existence, we encounter the ever-present specter of death. Yet, it is not to be feared but seen as a doorway to new beginnings.

To pass through this threshold, we must relinquish the physical vessel, releasing all attachments to worldly matters. The next destination awaits, always within reach, as our creations become a testament to the chapters we leave behind.

In this eternal dance of life and transition, we must grasp the profound truth of true ownership. It transcends material possessions and extends to the essence of being. Ownership is the summoning of the spirit that travels with us, igniting our souls with purpose and abundance.

Through this alchemical process, we unlock the riches of our existence.

You, dear soul, are the Avatar, the alchemist of your own destiny, the embodiment of the transformative forces within. Amidst the distractions of a driven world, my words may appear as detours leading you astray. But remember, when one is truly driven, they pursue their path by any means necessary, embracing the full spectrum of experiences.

Let us venture into the darkness together, recognizing that true companionship lies in the connection we forge with the divine and the collective spirit that surrounds us. Embrace the dance of life, surrender to the ever-flowing currents of change, and unlock the limitless potential that resides within your being."

—— · · ○ ☽ ☼ ☾ ○ · · ——

"Once touched or initiated, we can be victim, victimizer, or hero. There is always a choice. I pray through this inevitable battle, which most might encounter in some form or fashion, that the better part of you emerges."

Darnell P. Smith is a writer, poet, and truth-seeker whose work reflects a lifelong journey of

> *Please find the following points of connection as resources through your journey in self-discovery.*

transformation, resilience, and spiritual awakening. Shaped by the storms of his upbringing, he has navigated confusion, contradiction, and disconnection while continually searching for deeper meaning, belonging, and truth. From an early age, he questioned the narratives around him, sensing that something greater awaited beyond the masks society wears.

Guided by mentors, teachers, and his own inner compass, Darnell grew into a voice committed to **exploring identity, culture, justice, and the human condition.** His work speaks to the realities of struggle, the weight of history, and the pursuit of wholeness. At its heart, his writing is an offering— an illumination of the complexities of being, the necessity of connection, and the ongoing quest to understand our relationship with self, community, and Creator. Through his words,

Darnell invites readers to join him on a journey of reflection, awakening, and becoming. By weaving together reflections on spirit, culture, and the human condition, he invites readers to confront uncomfortable truths, seek clarity, and embrace the possibility of transformation.

To connect with Darnell, visit his websites below:

Substack:

darnellpsmith.substack.com/

Tik Tok:

@darnell.p..smith

Instagram:

@darnell.p.smith

Mahaba House Foundation is the institutional guardian of Mahaba House's mission.

A sacred healing space designed to serve and restore Black and Brown professionals and leaders who are committed to revolutionizing social impact and transforming lives to restore community.

Our mission is to radically heal and cultivate healthy, balanced leaders and communities.

Mahaba House Foundation is **deeply committed to building community through intentional investment in purpose-driven leadership.** At the core of our model is

co-creation—we believe in developing leaders personally and professionally by supporting their vision, nurturing their wellness, and walking beside them as they step into power. Through this approach, we cultivate a robust network of transformational leaders working collectively toward liberation, restoration, and equity.

"Mahaba" means **love** in Swahili. Leading with love, Mahaba House was established to **sustain, protect, and amplify the vision of communities committed to healing and liberation.** We invest in and uphold the organizations, businesses, and leaders who are building communities where Black and Brown professionals can restore, heal, and reclaim their power.

Steeped in African and Indigenous traditions, Mahaba House creates **sacred, trauma-informed, and culturally affirming healing spaces.** The organization is incorporated in New York with expansion efforts underway in the Eastern Caribbean with sights on Africa. Through the foundation, we ensure the longevity of a movement rooted in love, transformation, and collective well-being.

Our Co-Founders

- **Nicole W. Sharpe** — A seasoned nonprofit executive and strategist with a career dedicated to mobilizing philanthropy and advancing nonprofit practice throughout the Caribbean region. In a region where institutional philanthropy often overlooks needs beyond disaster relief, Nicole has championed long-term sustainability and equity. She is the author of *The Gift:*

Journal for Caribbean Philanthropy (Volumes I & II), which provides critical insights, best practices, and recommendations for institutional advancement, transparency, and capacity building in the region. Nicole can be reached at nicole@mahabahouse.com.

- **Kamau T. Ptah** — An expert rites-of-passage practitioner and educational consultant, Kamau brings decades of experience in youth development and community building. He is the author of *Crossing the Threshold, Embracing the Call: Conceptualizing, Co-Creating, and Building Community Through Rite of Passage*. His work, grounded in African and Indigenous traditions, shapes the foundation of Mahaba House's culturally affirming and healing-centered spaces. Kamau can be reached at akoben41@gmail.com.

Join Us

Mahaba House is a co-creation of **Caribbean Giving, Inc.** and **Akoben Enterprise.** Together, we joined in Spirit to lead with Love and to bring forth our best in establishing Mahaba House.

We invite you to **build with us**—to co-create the community you envision, to sustain healing spaces, and to strengthen a movement of love, transformation, and collective liberation.

Hailing from St. Thomas, Virgin Island, **Claudette Anita C'Faison** is a master at delivering **transformational and spiritual programs**. With a mission to bring healing to generational trauma and poverty, she leaves people empowered to create, and be accountable for, their reality and the lives they have made for themselves. For more than 40 years, she has made the difference for over 15,000 marginalized families and children, and counting, on every continent except Antarctica. In partnerships with family court, juvenile and adult justice programs, Claudette also creates and produces programs for inmates, returning citizens and children of incarcerated parents. She has been doing this work alongside her husband of 41 years.

She has been traditionally and non-traditionally

educated, completing the traditional path in seminary and being initiated to the non-traditional path in Ghana, Nigeria, Egypt and Peru. Her journey continues as she fulfills her life's purpose making a difference that makes the difference.

To connect with Claudette and her initiative NY Unlocking Futures, you can email <u>info@nyunlockingfutures.org</u> and visit **www.nyunlockingfutures.org**.

Chelsey Macklin is a writer, poet, author, mother of all, and founder of **RosePrayer Publishing,** a creative home dedicated to amplifying melanated voices through the written word. Her journey began with the self-publishing of her first poetry book in 2018, a process that sparked both a deep sense of accomplishment and a passion for guiding others in bringing their visions to life. After publishing a second book in 2020 and navigating the challenges of protecting her own intellectual property, Chelsey realized her calling: to **create a safe, empowering, and integrity-driven publishing space where writers are supported not only in manifesting**

their words into books but also in protecting their legacies.

Through RosePrayer Publishing and communal endeavors, Chelsey offers a wide range of services including writing workshops, literary resources, editing, publishing, and curated events, all **grounded in her devotion to preserving and elevating creative expression and self-development.** She believes that writing is both a sacred act and a channel for healing, authenticity, and imagination—an alchemical process that transforms emotion and vision into something eternal. Rooted in purpose, passion, and integrity, Chelsey is committed to helping people of all ages and stages honor their voices, protect their stories, and leave behind a trail of words and cultivate authentic souls that will echo for generations. Chelsey is also a proud member of Women's Press Collective, a women-led, all volunteer and non-government funded membership association in her hometown of the Bronx NY, dedicated to building independent press to tell the stories corporate media won't.

To contact Chelsey about services and be a part of her communities:

Email: inforoseprayer@gmail.com

Instagram:

@bytherosebush

@roseprayerpublishing

www.ingramcontent.com/pod-product-compliance
Lightning Source LLC
Chambersburg PA
CBHW060946050426
42337CB00052B/1618